Eyes

Julie Murray

Peachtree

abdopublishing.com

Published by Abdo Kids, a division of ABDO, PO Box 398166, Minneapolis, Minnesota 55439.
Copyright © 2016 by Abdo Consulting Group, Inc. International copyrights reserved in all countries.
No part of this book may be reproduced in any form without written permission from the publisher.

Printed in the United States of America, North Mankato, Minnesota.

102015

012016

 THIS BOOK CONTAINS RECYCLED MATERIALS

Photo Credits: iStock, Shutterstock

Production Contributors: Teddy Borth, Jennie Forsberg, Grace Hansen

Design Contributors: Candice Keimig, Dorothy Toth

Library of Congress Control Number: 2015941982

Cataloging-in-Publication Data

Murray, Julie.

 Eyes / Julie Murray.

   p. cm. -- (Your body)

ISBN 978-1-68080-158-3 (lib. bdg.)

Includes index.

1. Eye--Juvenile literature. 2. Vision--Juvenile literature.   I. Title.

612.8/4--dc23

                        2015941982

Table of Contents

Eyes

Eyes are a part of your body.

You have two eyes.

Eyes allow you to see.

Mary sees a boat.

You can see color.

Amy sees a red bike.

You can see shapes.

Lily sees a round ball.

Some eyes are brown.

Some are blue or green.

You can **blink** your eyes.

You close your eyes to sleep.

Some people can't see well.

Jimmy wears **glasses**.

Animals have eyes too.

Owls have big eyes!

What color are your eyes?

21

Parts of the Eye

Eyelid

Pupil

Iris

Sclera

Glossary

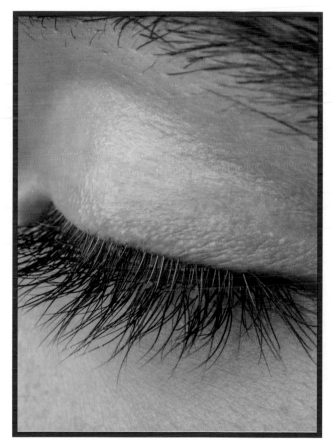

blink
to open and close your eyes quickly.

glasses
an item that helps people see.

Index

abdokids.com

Use this code to log on to abdokids.com and access crafts, games, videos, and more!

Abdo Kids Code:
YEK1583